A White Christmas

Two Tales of Ghetto Cheer

A White Christmas

In two weird urban tales, the author of a Hoodrat Halloween, Skulker Jones and Hurt Stoker continues as the only authentic storyteller for a masculine tradition which no literary faction wishes to know the truth about.

In Trinity, the three sons of Trinity Baxter are sent out by their mother to rob some white people in order to finance her Christmas feast, even as the supernatural specter of a gang of Caucasian rats haunts their every defiant step.

In The Song of Broke-Ass Rasheed, the wheelchair-bound elder statesman of a liquor store front mourns the death of the crew he had previously served as mentor and at the same time is called upon to advise the young hoppers who mean to step-up and take their place as gangbangers in their own right.

Books by James LaFond

Nonfiction
The Fighting Edge, 2000
The Logic of Steel, 2001
The First Boxers, 2011
The Gods of Boxing, 2011
All Power Fighting, 2011
When You're Food, 2011
The Lesser Angles of Our Nature, 2012
The Logic of Force, 2012
The Greatest Boxer, 2012
Take Me to Your Breeder, 2014
The Streets Have Eyes, 2014
Panhandler Nation, 2014
The Ghetto Grocer, 2014
American Fist, 2014
Don't Get Boned, 2014
Alienation Nation, 2014
In The Chinks of The Machine, 2014
How the Ghetto Got My Soul, 2014
Saving the World Sucks, 2014
Taboo You, 2014
Winter of a Fighting Life, 2014

Narco Night Train, 2014
Into the Mountains of Madness: in [3 volumes], 2014
Incubus of Your Sacred Emasculation, 2014
Breeder's Digest, 2014
The Third Eye, 2015
Modern Agonistics, 2015
By the Wine Dark Sea, 2015
The Pale Usher, 2016
The End of Masculine Time, 2015
War Drums, 2015
A Thousand Years in His Soul: The Poets, 2015
A Thousand Years in His Soul: The Seers, 2015
Of Lions and Men, 2015
Your Trojan Whorse, 2016
On Bitches, 2016
Equidistant Drowning Babies, 2015
The Boned Zone, 2015
A Sickness of the Heart: Part One, 2015
Let the Weak Fall, 2015
If I Were King, 2015
Dark Art of an Aryan Mystic, 2015
Welcome to Harm City: White Boy, 2015
When You're Food: Raw, 2016
The Punishing Art, 2016
Twerps, Goons and Meatshields, 2016
Our Captain, 2016
Stillbirth of A Nation, 2016
America in Chains, 2106
40,000 Years from Home, 2016
The Sardonyx Stone, 2017
Paleface Sunset, 2016
Habitat Hoodrat: Ho Nation, 2016
When Your Job Sucks, 2016
A Once Great Medieval City, 2016
Right on White Time, 2016

A Well of Heroes: One, 2016
A Well of Heroes: Two, 2016
Thriving in Bad Places, 2016
Into Wicked Company, 2016
One Soul Under God, 2016
Under the God of Things, 2016
When Your Job Sucks, 2016
Dawn in Dindustan, 2016
Good Morning Dindustan, 2016
The Hunt for Whitey, 2017
Habitat Hoodrat: Yo Nation, 2016
The Combat Space, 2017
A Dread Grace: One, 2017
The Liver-Eater Reader, 2017
Rubbing Out palefaces, 2017
In Words, 2017
Slave Nation, 2016
I Am White, 2017
The Lies that Bind Us, 2017
Real Heroes, 2017
Aryan Myth, 2017
Why Grownups Suck, 2017
A Dread Grace: Two, 2017
A Well of Heroes: Three, 2017
The Boxer Dread, 2017

Fiction
Astride the Chariot of Night, 2014
Sacrifix, 2014
Rise, 2014
Motherworld, 2014
Planet Buzzkill, 2014
Fruit of The Deceiver, 2014
Forty Hands of Night, 2014
Black and Pale, 2014

Daughters of Moros, 2014
Darkly, 2014
This Design is Called Paisley, 2015
Hurt Stoker, 2015
Poet, 2016
Triumph, 2015
Winter, 2015
The Spiral Case, 2016
Hemavore, with S. L. James, 2016
Yusuf of the Dusk, 2017
Beyond the Pale, 2017
RetroGenesis: Day 1, with Erique Watson, 2015
Easy Chair, 2015
Happily Ever Under, 2015
Road Killing, 2015
Fat Girl Dancing, 2015
Buzz Bunny, 2015
T. Spoone Slickens, Inquire, 2015
Dream Flower, 2015
The Song of Jeannot, 2015
Organa, 2015
A Hoodrat Halloween, 2015
Buzz Bunny, 2015
The Consultant, 2015
Reverent Chandler, 2015
He, 2016
Little Feet Going Nowhere, 2016
DoomFawn, 2016
The Jericho Bone, 2016
Ire and Ice, 2016
Night City, 2016
Skulker Jones, 2016
A White Christmas, 2016
Night Song of the Nords, 2017
The Absolvant, 2017

Wendigo, 2017
Sold, 2017
Bad Medicine, 2018
Kettle of Bones, 2019

Sunset Saga Novels
Big Water Blood Song, 2011
Ghosts of the Sunset World, 2011
Beyond the Ember Star, 2012
Comes the Six Winter Night, 2012
Thunder-Boy, 2012
The World is Our Widow, 2013
Behind the Sunset Veil, 2013
Den of The Ender, 2013
God's Picture Maker, 2014
Out of Time, 2015
Seven Moons Deep, 2016
WhiteSkyCanoe, 2017

A White Christmas

For Big Sam, who died in a ghetto alley one wintry night.

Table of Contents

Trinity

A White Christmas

Written while listening to Wongraven—Fjelltronen, available at the link below and via the window at the bottom of the page:

https://www.youtube.com/watch?v=jocdubzSPXU

Anno Domini 2022, Christmas Eve, Saturday, December 24, 11:30 a.m., Park Heights and Belvedere, West Baltimore, Maryland

The Sons of Trinity Baxter

    It was cold in the house, the icy winter air whistling in through the trash bags taped to the window frame above him. His bed was pretty warm though, with only his face getting cold from where it peeked out from underneath the knit hat and the vast pile of clothes he had burrowed under.

It was barely light and something was scratching at the window, and something else was dropping on his chin—crumbs?

Traymore looked up in the early morning half-light and saw Jesse, the Boss rat, the one that wasn't afraid, eating a Pop Tart from a perch on the old coat he was nestled under, right over where his hands were tucked on his chest. Jesse was looking right in his eyes—a rat the size of the cats they used to have, before the cats was driven out by the rats.

Jesse, named after Jesse James because he was a damned near white city rat, simply looked into Traymore's eyes as he nibbled on the Pop Tart. Traymore did not like to be awoked before noon, and was right mad, exclaiming as he flicked at Jesse's feet from beneath the coat, "Get the fuck off, Jesse!" to which the rat bounded away over the pile of old clothes that was the bed for Traymore and his two dumbass brothers.

Traymore kicked out under the heaped clothes and caught Trayvon in the ribs.

"Ouch, Yo," came the muffled protest.

"Trayvon, you dumbass lead-eaten muvafuca, Yo cain't be eatin in bed. It encourages Jesse. Before you know it he'll have the whole James Gang up in here eatin' our frozen asses in our sleep!"

Trayvon simply curled deeper into the abyss of old clothes and new donated clothes that filled half of this room and made for a cozy bed. Then Trayserious barked, "Yo, you interrupted a good dream, Nigga!" and konked Traymore on the head with one of the boots they had stole from Trinity's man's car while he was up in her bedroom making time.

The three brothers were now good and awake and began getting their shit together for the day. Traymore's warning that Jesse and the James Gang might soon be driving them out, like they had them Siamese Bitchez, had struck a note in their minds and they all started pulling together. The first order of business was selecting what parts of the bed should form Trayvon's outfit for the day, with Traymore sniffing the air to determine the temperature and Trayserious doing most of Trayvon's dressing. Trayvon was slow, "had the lead" from eating window paint and was not as smart as Trayserious, who was not that smart to begin with. Traymore, though the middle brother at 10 years, was essentially the leader. Trasereus, at twelve, was their lead on the street. Trayvon was just, well, Trayvon—"got-the-lead" Trayvon, which had got Trinity all of her nice shit like the BMW and the pink silk canopy over her bed, and all the weed she smoked and liquor she drank with her mens.

Trayvon was also responsible for Traymystery's high living; her dresses, weaves, braids, her going to private school. So Trinity and their older sister had benefitted greatly from Trayvon's affliction caused by the evil lead paint made by those white companies that ran the world and kept a nigga down. However, this high standard of living did not reach to the Sons of Trinity Baxter who were charged primarily with looking after one another. Traymore had been looking after Trayvon since he was old enough to remember—five he was when he became the babysitter, cause Trayserious was so busy beatin' the mess outta other niggas they age.

So here they was, getting dressed from the donated clothes pile in the crumbledown room at the back of the old house where the windswept up from the highway where the distant white people zoomed their cars to wherever it was they went, from whence ever they came.

All dressed warm now, the three boys walked down the long hall, past the bathroom with the cardboard window, where that crackhead had once crawled into to die on a previous Christmas. This had freaked Trinity out, so she had made Traymore responsible for checking the bathroom and Trayserious responsible for laying the steel pipe he carried into crackhead heads when they came near the house. In a creepy kind of way, the crackheads were beginning to become like the rats, only not as intelligent.

The sons of Trinity Baxter did swagger a bit as they walked down the hall to the game room where Trinity's man sat smoking weed, drinking a forty, and playing a video game in his gay-looking bathrobe and sweat pants bottoms. Traymore swore that one day he would stuff a sock down this man's throat while he slept, for the man had struck him once for back-sassing Trinity, who needed some back-sassing on occasion on account of her being a stupid bitch.

The scent of the 'stupid smoke,' as he called what all adults seemed to be addicted to in their dumbass way, assaulted his senses, made Trayvon sneeze, and made Trayserious start to nod. He knew that one day he would have to deal with Trayserious getting hooked on weed and often wondered what he would do about that.

Trinity's man looked at them and said, "What up, lille Gs."

Traymore wasn't in the mood for this shit after being awoked by Jesse James, so he snapped back, "Fuck you, nigger."

The man got up and came heavy stalking toward Traymore, who stood his ground with his hand on his razor deep in the pocket of his Washington Redskins starter jacket. The man hovered over him menacingly, dropping the controller and making to grab Traymore's neck between his massive hands, and snarled, "Who you callin' nigger, you little nigglet?"

Traymore stood tall, to the man's belly button, "You, nigger."

The man then took Traymore's neck between his hands as he had known he would. As he lifted Traymore off the tarpaper floor Traymore slid his razor out and slashed the inside of the man's wrist to the guitar strings, which caused Trinity Baxter's latest man to take a knee, whining like a bitch, while he pressed one hand to the other wrist, and Trayserious smacked the side of his big pumpkin head with his galvanic steel pipe, which they had named Galvanic Lightning, their unrustable talisman.

Traymore then took Lilly, his straight razor, and slashed the man's junk through his sweat pants and the big dude ran crashing out the front door into the middle of the street screaming like bitch. The boys closed the door behind him and divided up his shit, including a plastic baggie with some money and weed in it.

As they stood over the place where the man had camped out on the old, dirty, cigarette-burned couch, Trayserious downing the rest of that warm forty of Steel Reserve malt liquor, they heard Trinity emerge in a loud rage from Traymystery's room where she usually braided her daughter's hair, her nightgown flapping around all unseemly and whatnot.

"What are you evil little niggas doin'?— where my mans at!"

They all three looked up at their mother, all looking back at her like indicting ghosts cast up from the hell where their various anonymous fathers surely resided by now.

Trayvon did what he always did when he got in trouble, putting his finger to his enlarged lower lip and rapping, "I got da lead. I got da lead!"

Trayserious, Galvanic Lightning in one hand and a bottle of malt liquor still draining down his throat from the bottle held high in the other hand, just drank his drink until it was drunk dry.

Traymore, having slyly pocketed his razor, as was his method after dealing with these miserable adults, just deadlocked Trinity in the eyes and lied convincingly, "Nigger laid a hand on Trayvon."

Her fury abated somewhat, Trinity then put her meaty fists to meatier hips and bobbled her head, saying, "Then you niggas need to get Mamma some scrimps, some snow crab clusters and a Christmas cake—which dat nigga was goin' ta do today, and ain't ever gonna do now!"

Her finger, tipped with a swirl of exotic hand-painted color, then bent angrily out at the world and she snarled, "Then ya'all get out en don' come back 'till you done got that hundred en fitty dolla's wort a Christmas—go waylay some white people if ya have to—but don't come back in here unless you mens enough to replace the mans you run off!"

They all three nodded obediently, Trayvon saying, "Get da lead out, get da lead out," Trayserious belching, and Traymore saying, "Yes, Mamma—we gotchyou."

So, out into the cold cruel world trekked the three Sons of Trinity Baxter, with but six hours to make enough money to buy Trinity and Traymystery they Christmas Eve dinner.

As they walked down toward Park Heights Traymore took out the bag of weed, separated it for sale at the liquor mart—which would bring a hundred—and counted out the cash as the two other brothers gathered around.

Trayserious mumbled, "How much da big nigga have?"

"Shit, dat fool bitch Trinity weren't gettin shit from dis nigga—but sixty-two beans. Dis en da weed gets us our good time. Let's go get Trinity and Traymystery dey good time."

Out onto Park Heights they walked, the Sons of Trinity Baxter, at war with an old, cold world.

Nine

A White Christmas: Winter, Addendum, Part Two

With Traymore in the lead, hands pocketed in his heretical Washington Redskins starter jacket, Trayvon following in his slouching gait, mumbling in his lead-paint-eating way, and Trayserious towering behind, swinging his left hand, and holding Galvanic Lightning—his trusty, steel crack-head-splitting pipe—in the right palm and up the sleeve of his puff coat, the Sons of Trinity Baxter walked across Belvedere, past the closed-down lake trout joint, and across Park Heights to the Liquor Mart.

In front of the Liquor Mart, as the stinging wet snow began to bite like Jesse James the Rat on crack, the three boys, 12-dumbass hard-fightin' years, 10 smart-fucking years, and 8-lead-eatin' years of age respectably, they came to a halt before the elder stewards of their world, the badass gangbangers of park heights, The SSH [Send-you-to-Sinai-Hospital] Crew:

Trayserious curled his lip and grasped Galvanic lightning as he came nose to nose with Pinkie Rotgun, who posed menacingly.

Trayvon began drooling a big snot string and rapping up into Milkdud Johnson's wide face, "Get-out-da-lead, get-out-da-lead." Mildud was so worried about snot getting on his vintage Jack Percels that he kept stepping away and around, making for an unseemly sight.

Traymore stepped up in a more considered manner before muscled-up Nine, who was the man who ran this hood, from this liquor store front—a bad enough dude that he didn't even have a government name attached to his street name any more. Traymore knew better than to get rancid with this dude and waited respectfully, hands in pockets, the right one on Lilly, the junk slicing razor-bitch from hell, for Nine to speak.

After a tense moment Nine spoke, "Yo, More, call off you lead-eatin' brutha, en tell Serious to keep dat pipe up he sleeve."

Traymore nodded to his brothers and they both went inside to shop for breakfast, Milkdud and Pinkie Rotgun looking all relieved and whatnot.

Traymore and Nine then backed into the doorway shoulder to shoulder and looked out at the rotten world, hands in pockets by default, only producing them for business of one sort or another. Nine was dressed in tight jeans, longhorn boots and a leather jacket over a hoody.

Nine: "You niggas is somethin' else—saw Trinity's man runnin' down the way to Sinai leakin' from the groans and the guitar strings. Whatchyou got dat shit in you pocket for me too, gonna cut old Nine up wit dat bitch blade?"

Traymore: "Naw, G, got dat nigga's bag a weed, wan a hundred for it."

Nine: "Shit, nigga, I just' sold it to the fool fo one-fitty yesterday! Why I wan' that shit back? What you need that kinna money fo anyhow. Yo brutha gots the lead—you all should be set."

Traymore: "Oh, you know how it be, Trinity keep all that shit fo her en Traymystery en her mens. En after the cuttin' of the junk she sent us out to get her Christmas present."

Nine: "Now, Nine is willing to help a little brutha out, but I don't buy my own shit back—a matter of principal, don't you know. So what else you got for Nine, yo?"

The jangle of keys got Nine's attention as Traymore jingled them in his face with his left hand. "Trinity's junk-cut man lef' his truck up the way. Here are the keys—chop dat shit up, yo!"

Nine reached for the keys and they disappeared into Traymore's pocket.

Nine quipped, "Nigga, you gettin' out of yo league. I thought you was just lookin' fo Trinity's Christmas present?"

Traymore: "Kinna hard to get Mamma her Christmas present when a cheap nigga don' wanna deal!"

Nine opened his mouth to speak in a defensive manner and was cutoff when an old gravelly voice rudely interrupted them, "What you hoppers know about a deal, or about Christmas fo that matter? Riddle me that, young poke eaters, riddle me that!"

Broke-Ass Rasheed

A White Christmas: Winter, Addendum, Part Three

The decrepit figure of Broke-Ass Rasheed wheeled up on his power chair, putting the one stiff leg of his that was strapped into the iron boot between the two power players, taking over the conversation as if it were his, looking obstinately from player to player from beneath his gray brows and above his steel wool-looking beard, and then repeating his question, or reformulating it rather, as the bells he wore all year long on his Nation of Islam flag and his Black Panther beret jingled in the cold, snow-spitting wind, "Riddle me that, Hoppers, what a poke-eatin' set a fools like you know 'bout Christmas, let alone Jew-Christmas?"

Nine retorted, "At least we celebrate that shit, Broke-Ass, not like you with yo militant, rice-eatin' bullshit."

Milkdud laughed out loud, only to be scolded by Broke-Ass Rasheed, who spared him not a look, but pointed the finger of blind disdain back over his shoulder in that direction, "At least a White Devil didn't plant his vile seed up in my mamma and spawn a Lionel Richie lookin' somebody!"

They all laughed at that, even Milkdud, who shook his head with a smile. With this approval, the man who once ran this corner "way back in the old-ass day," now reduced to an advisor/mascot of the SSH Crew, who he admonished weekly—sometimes daily—for eating pork rinds and drinking liquor, continued. In truth, though a not often heeded advisor, Broke-Ass Rasheed was more than a mascot to the SSH Crew, for whom he served as a sort of social shield, as the crew could always pretend to be helping Rasheed or listening to his sidewalk sermons whenever the po-leese rolled on by.

His sermonious voice mixed with the patter of the wet snow and rose above their laughs and chuckles, "Yo all think my ass don't know what goin' on up in here? The Sons of Trinity Baxter—who I done gave bubblegum to on this very spot right before the Hugo-North boys sprayed all that lead into my black ass—are headin' out to make their mamma's Christmas wishes come true. Ain't it so, More?" Rasheed said, looking straight into Traymore's eyes from his power chair.

Not having realized until now, that he had been honored with a street name at such a young age, Traymore nodded "Yes," and stood defiantly.

The old power-chair preacher in the black felt beret gave a studied wink and declared, "I thought you would be the one. You Umari Stackhouse's son—destined ta lead. "

Broke-Ass Rasheed then looked to Nine and said, "Treat him right, Nine."

Traymore was in a head spin. He had always been able to figure things out and see them coming. But this, this news that someone knew who his father was—that he had a father, had not been bought at the Baby Mart—struck him like a wind striking a falling candy wrapper. He wanted to ask questions, find out what happened to the man that fathered him, but Broke-Ass Rasheed was lecturing him.

"You young hoppers probably figuring on walkin' out to Jew Town and rob you a Jew, get you some of that money that Satan done set them up with for managing the enslavement of the Black Man on behalf of the earthly White Devil Incarnate—it's the curse of Yakub and not a thing can be done about it, 'cept fight back and subterfugate the situation.

"Let me tell you about Jew Christmas, son, it called Harmony, a candle lit each day for a week to mark each millennium—that's not a million years, like some dumbass niggas might think, but a thousand—of the Black Man's bondage, the bondage that done deposited yo soul-starved ass on this abandoned white man stoop. These Jews got so much shit, and is so good at hiding it, working through they Korean front men and sucking up to Whitey, they ration out they Christmas. Sho, they might be an easy mark, but they too sly with they ill-gotten goods to be caught with much by a righteous redistributing brutha like you. So, what I be sayin' is, though waylayin' a Hebrew is equivalent to African retribution, it ain't gonna get you shit.

Besides, they got they own Jew Pol-eese—they own desk officer at the precinct, mannin'—or Devillin,' rather—the Jew Phone! Naw, naw, Little Brutha, Jew Town ain't fo you, not 'till you get a car. What you want is to get yo hard-scrappin' self down the way en get you the first white 'block buster' you can. Can you believe that they come callin' themselves 'block busters' when they move their rich asses back into the hood that their granddaddys' narrow asses vacated? It is an affront, I tell you, a stick in the eye!"

Broke-Ass Rasheed sat, woolly chin jutting, good hand pointing firmly, back down into the hood behind the Mattress Street and the Dice Way, the Flat House Lot and the Ghost Apartments, as if envisioning a great big house full of rich, scared-ass white folks ready to hand over all of they stacks of money and their sweet-ass rides rather then throw down.

There was an ominous and respectful pause of awed silence—most of all by the way-pointing speaker.

"Go there, Young G, bring the Inextinguishable Spirit of Africa into the heart of Whitey's regurgitude, and get you a White Christmas down in there. They are there, ask your brother here."

With that, Broke-Ass Rasheed motored off on his quiet wheels in the spitting snow and Traymore looked up accusingly at Nine, who had a haunted look in his eyes. "You didn't tell me about no polar bears hidin' out up in here?"

Nine was hesitant, "Look, it's projects for white retards, okay, white people with fucked up brains. Broke-Ass dere is jus' pissed he didn't get one a dose free joints for he own self—still livin' with his sista—and she a straight-up, giant, scary bitch!"

Traymore knew his place now, new that he was somebody's son, felt there was a purpose behind his big-ass brain, and looked up coldly into the eyes of Nine—kind of pissed that he had never told him that they had the same father, though this might explain his patronage—who seemed unsteady, not his normal cool-dealing self.

"Nine, how comes you put up with Broke-Ass Rasheed busting yo nuts up here, in your joint?"

Nine answered in a subdued voice, "When I was a little rip-en-runner like you, he treated me right. So I treat him right. I respect him."

It was time to pounce. Holding out the car keys he announced, "I'll smoke yo weed for wasting my time, en you can have this car for that spare iron you keep up behind that brick there," pointing with his chin to where Nine kept his palm gun, the .25 auto.

Nine's eyes bugged out in surprise, "Nigga, why should I even entertain that shit?"

For answer Traymore, nodded to the now distant form of Broke-Ass Rasheed, making his bitter Broke-Ass way across Park Heights in the snow, subject to the kindness of strangers in cars, and said, "One day, when Broke-Ass Nine wans ta be heard from that wheelie chair he be stuck in, maybe I'll listen, maybe I'll treat him right, maybe I'll respect him."

Nine looked down into him like he had just seen his own death, shivered, and reached for the loose brick. As keys and gun exchanged hand in the snow-pelted doorway of the Liquor Mart and Milkdud made way for Trayvon and Trayserious,

Nine said to him icily, "More, you a evil little muthafucka already, en the only reason I do this is 'cause we got da same daddy—en you didn't hear that shit from me. Now get on wit your hard-dealin' self. Go on, More, go get you mamma her White Christmas!"

More flashed hard eyes up at Nine and then pocketed *his* first G-iron, a warrior now, before his years, heading out to pop the shit-dealing White World in the eye.

As giddy with confidence as he now felt with a gun in his pocket, as justifiably angry as he felt at Trinity for hiding the fact that his daddy was some big-time badass, and as warm as he felt over discovering that Nine was his for-real-flesh-and-blood-brother, Traymore-no-more, but More, was nervous about the prospect of hunting around behind the Ghost Apartments, the very same place where that dopefiend that Trayserious had head-smashed had crawled, never to be seen again, not even strapped to a po-leese wheelie-bed with a sheet over his dead ass.

But with Trayvon acting the fool, and Trayserious looking leaderless and confused, he was soon out of that care-taking place that remained way in the back of his brain, and stepped back up to the front of life and declared, "We goin' huntin' down behind the Ghost Apartments for Broke-Ass Rasheed's block busters!"

Trayserious nodded silently and clenched his jaw and Trayvon rapped, "Get out da lead, get out da lead!"

The wind shifted, got a bite colder, and drove the ice crystals of some white man's idea of a nice Christmas into their faces, the hoods over their heads merely managing to funnel the icy, wet mess into their eyes.

Da Weird-Ass White-Boy

A White Christmas: Winter, Addendum, Part Three

The air was cold for a Christmas lunchtime, not that More had experienced many Christmas lunchtimes, but is was twelve mufafucking-a'clock and the sun should be shinin' or some shit! As they made their way back past the weed-grown house that Stiff-ass Yarbow share with his grandmamma—which was some ridiculous shit being as he was a granddaddy his own self—the Dice Alley came in sight through the blistering ice that was frosting the rims of their hoodys, 'cause every serious little nigga wear a hoody under his brand apparel jacket in case of police cameras, which also covered you for this kind of shit.

They worked their way to the Dice Alley and weren't Stiff-ass Yarbow, Grimy Old Mofo, Blisterpack, Coochie Moochie, or any of those old-ass dudes rolling they dice back this way, *not today, no wonder with this cold mess coming down slant ways.*

Just then Trayvon spoke up, "I got da lead, I got da lead!"

More and Trayserious looked at their slow-ass brother and saw him pointing two some dice, and some quarters and one dollar bills in the dice rolling box, as well as a pack of cigarettes laying as if some old mofos had been scared off by cops and the cops were so lame that they didn't pocket that good shit when they seen it. Trayvon picked up the cash, the cigarettes, the quarters, and grabbed for the dice—and something streaked at his hand.

More drew his razor—not yet practiced with the palm gun—and Trayserious whipped out

Galvanic Lightning. That's when they all noticed that Trayvon was not being attacked. Trayserious was the first to speak—which was unusual "Jesse James, what da fo, yo?"

The large, white-ass rat with the black marks around his eyes and brown-fringed mouth and legs had picked up one dice and was dropping it gingerly into Trayvon's open palm, with the cash, as the ice pelted them all. Trayvon was in ecstasy, a wide smile on his face and chortled, "Get out da lead!"

The rat then picked up the other dice—a rat every bit as big as a cat—and looked up into Trayvon's eyes, then into Trayserious' eyes, and finally stared at More for a long moment, and turned, lopping off out of the Dice Way, and across the Flat House Lot—all weeds and bottles and whatnot—to the Mattress Street.

"We need ta follow, yo, let's go," More said, as he pocketed Lily and darted off after Jesse James, who was more than a dice stealing rat, but a smart gangster somebody.

The crunching of broken bottles and crispy ice coated grass—for it had been icing back here on the Flat House Lot longer than out on the street where they come from—broke the spitting breeze sound and gave them more confidence. Suddenly, as they were halfway across the field that used to be a home, Jesse James leaped high over something onto the Mattress Street and stopped looking back at him from his two hind feet, and then heading off down the street toward the Ghost Apartment, behind which the street bent crookedly.

More encouraged his men, "Come on, yo, Jesse James is leadin' us to some shit, let's move!"

They broke into a ragged run, which ended suddenly as they found themselves at the edge of the lot, standing over Coochie Moochie, laying there terrified and shaking, his big blood shot eyes rolling in his drunk-ass head, mumbling something at them.

More shouted, Moochie, get da fuck out a here, and kicked the old drunk in the belly, the other boys following in kind, dancing round him to one side, laying in kicks until the old drunk crawled in the icy snow to his hands and knees and staggered off toward Park Heights. The deed done, More could tell that the others felt kind of bad about it, so he bucked up their spirits.

"Nine say you gotta whip an ole mofo dat sleepin' on yo street or he'll die up in there and bring the po-leese. Besides its fo his own mofo good, yo—after Jesse James!"

The icy snow was blowing in a torrent as they ran down the Mattress Street in pursuit of the tiny figure of Jesse James bounding in the distance, now lost to sight behind the Ghost Apartments.

They all gritted their teeth and toughed it out as they ran around the haunted dope-fiend death place, which was most certainly crawling with some kind of Lord of the Rings bullshit.

A White Christmas

In seconds they were behind the deserted apartments where they said that evil old white people had once lived like ghosts, skulking about with their evil ways in the unlit night, wearin' they hospital sheets like hoods. To the left way, on the other side of the unused parking lot was a mess of ivy-covered trees and wooden light poles without lights, whatever they were used for—*probably set up as police spy camera places way back in the old-ass day when cameras were real big.*

More could tell now that the snowy ice was not coming down on the other side of the trees, and, in fact, was pretty much just coming down over the lot, the Mattress Street, and real heavy back in here, behind this old brick building with its own parking lot, where they had once played in the big puddle, floating beer cans and vodka bottles and bombing them with rocks like they was army boats in war at sea.

Kneeling over the puddle now, with just a white people button shirt and jeans on, was a skinny big-headed white boy with straight black hair like a Mexican, sailing an actual plastic army boat out into the big-ass puddle.

"This is the chump, yo. Serious, watch our back. Trayvon, with me."

More strode out onto the lot, up to the chump white retard with his big head where he was perched, kneeling like some weird-ass faggot that never got beat when he was a kid by his ho mamma's mens!

The storm thundered in More's mind as he walked up to the retarded faggot and drew his razor and gun, raising the gun to the retard's face as it turned and looked up into his eyes, with eyes that seemed like they should belong to an adult, eyes that stung like needles in More's soul, which drove him to thrust out the gun for emphasis—then Trayvon got in the way, stepping right over to the retard and fouling More's aim.

"Von, what- da-fuck, yo?!"

Trayvon turned and smiled, pointing at the toy army boat, which had Jesse James' dice on it, "A voat, Vore, a voat!"

It was stunning to hear Trayvon say a word pretty close to true that wasn't 'get out,' 'I got', or 'the lead.'

Then, like in some gay fucking YouTube commercial about people that should be hating on each other inexplicably getting along, Trayvon held out his dice to the weird-ass white-boy and More tried to halt this unseemly ebony and ivory bullshit, as Broke-ass Rasheed would have called it.

"Von, don't give him yo dice."

Both of the retards then turned and looked at him as one, and Von said the first smart thing he had ever said in his life, only it didn't make sense, "It's a die, More, the singular form of the noun for this random number-generating cube. So, we play dice with dice, but this is a die. So when Caesar was about to cross the Rubicon he quoted from a play by Menander to say 'let the die be cast,' meaning one, and since it all did not work out precisely as he wished, and Virtius here is a big Caesar fan, he wanted to use two die—so that we would have a bell-shaped probability curve rather than a flat one—to cross this Rubicon, meaning dice, get it, more?"

"What-da-fuck, yo?" More said dumfounded.

Then, across the gathering snow that was whitening the dark lot, he heard a growl and a grunted, "More!"

Looking right he saw Serious seeming like he was falling down the stairs to the basement of the ancient building feet first, waving his pipe, and heard Von say in an emotionless manner, as he and the white retard began attending to the boat and dice together, "Sounds like Serious just met Pluto. Pluto plays for keeps. Yo might want to sort that out...yo."

Brain burning with impatience for retards of all colors, lead eating or not, family included, More sprinted for his older brother, who was being tugged roughly down the stairs by something unseen.

"Crack with Galvanic Lightning, Serious!"

Down with the James Gang

A White Christmas: Winter, Addendum, Part Five

More ran as hard as he could into the teeth of the stinging ice spit and saw Serious disappear down the stairwell, except for his one empty hand, which momentarily clutched at the base of the rusted out railing, and then was ripped away with a crack.

"No!" More raged as he came to the top of the stairwell and looked down, to see that it went deeper than it should.

45

The base of the stair was there, and so was Serious, being chewed on by a huge pitbull, dragged through crumbled brick and broken malt liquor bottles. Serious was looking up at More, and when he saw him, a light lit in his eye, just as the dog, when it saw More, looked up at him and slacked it's jaw grip just a little.

Inspired by More's appearance at the head of the stair, Serious struck like there was lightning in that Galvanic Steel pipe, the sound of the unbendable pipe making a "konk" sound on the meaty head of the dog, who loosened its grip just enough for Serious to yank his leg, leaving shredded pants and shoe in its mouth.

"Scamper, Serious, crawl liker you on crack!" More said as he pocketed Lilly and stepped down a few stairs and reached out his hand to his brother, all the while looking with terror, not on the ferocious dog, but on the jagged black stairway that extended below what used to be the bottom of this stairway when they came back her at the end of summer, but which now seemed a cavern chewed up from underground by something that made tiny scratches, not deep cuts in the dark earth.

As their grip tightened from wrist to wrist and More hooked his gun hand around the railing bar, the dog, who had paused, seemingly for this moment, pounced on Serious and bit hard into his scraped leg, champing down on the bone with a throaty growl of yummy triumph, like Trinity hopping on a cheese steak sub.

"Oh, hell no!" Serious moaned, as he was yanked back down onto the landing. More had the choice of staying put or being dragged with him, and he defiantly decided to be dragged along with his brother, unhooking his gun arm and taking the back-crunching head-cracking drag down the stairs.

More was no on the bottom stair, Serious laid flat-out at the base, with one foot in the mouth of the dog, whose entire body was down below on some crude chopped stairs, ready to tug them both down to hell.

Serious looked into his eyes and cried, "Save you self, yo—go, git!"

The dog seemed to be listening to Serious, waiting for More's answer before it gave that final, fateful tug, which lit a fire in More's mind as he pointed his gun at the wide dog face—black and gray and red in the half-dark—and snarled, "Put yo head down, Serious," and squeezed off a cap into that big fat head, a cap that just zinged off the thick skull and tore through the ear.

The beast, barely stunned, gave a mighty tug and dragged them, as More popped off his second cap and the .25 auto exploded in his hand, burning his fingers all to shredded shit and blinding Serious, who now moaned like a bitch as they were dragged.

The dog was now out of sight except for its snout, Serious was only out of the cave from the waist up, and More's head was bouncing off the bottom step.

When More felt Serious give up, a blinding rage swept through him and he pulled back his remaining hand—afraid to even look at what had become of his gun hand—and whipped out Lilly, diving headfirst into the cave mouth to slash that muthafuckin' pit's throat!

"Bitch!" screamed More, as he dove over his brother and came face-to-face with the pit, who still had Serious' ankle in his mouth. The nightmare seen was greyly illuminated, from above, as More lay face-first down in this cave-like stairway slicing that snout above the teeth, trying to carve them teeth out of that snarling face, since he could not get at the throat due to his brother's leg.

The dog just looked back hard in his eyes and dragged his brother down another step as his gums splashed blood across the way, causing some of the snowflakes floating in to blink red and disappear. It was getting dark and that was panicking More.

"Serious, break out dat nigga's lighter, yo. Lay some light down in here!"

As Serious was dragged down another step and More kept cutting, riding on his brother like he was a piece of cardboard used to slide down the snowy hillside at Cylburn. Down they went, both of them all the way in the deep hole, able to see nothing. Then—amidst the snarl of the tugging dog—came the flick of that Bic, the warmth behind his ear from the illuminating flame that would make his triumph possible and—

—There was Jesse James, glaring at him from atop the bloody dog's head, with the whole mothafuckin' James gang riding on the back of that dog, and a thousand red-eyed friends crowding the darkness behind. More's temper had not yet been extinguished, nor his spirit, as he pointed his blood-slick razor in the boss rat's face and swore, "Jesse, you ain't nothin' but a muthafuckin' hoodrat!"

With those words he and Serious were dragged down the dark dismal rat-chattering way, with Jesse James and one of his G-rats taking away Lily in the waving light of the flame as the dog snarled and hauled, and a hundred sharp-toed feet leaped upon his back as the light went out and warm, greasy bodies began worming up into his sleeves and pants legs.

As the rough-cut stair gave way to a rat-shit ramp, the cold of winter soon gave way to a pulsing warmth, a warmth that did not warm the hearts of Traymore and Trayserious Baxter, at lunchtime, on a white Christmas.

"Jesse!"

A White Christmas

The Song of Broke-Ass Rasheed

Another White Christmas

Every warrior society has its shaman, soothsayer, wise man, or witchdoctor to consult before going on a quest. It's no different for the Park Heights crew. Three innocent, unarmed youth find themselves in need of a white Christmas. The only problem is, them white people just keep moving farther and farther away. So, once the boyz tool up with razors and guns—still unarmed, don't you know—to go hunting for their mamma's Christmas scrimp feast, they find themselves in need of wisdom:

Snickarius – 14 young-ass years old, tall and lanky with two razors stolen from each of his sisters' wigs, is ready to hunt whitey but don't know where he's at.

Jamalabad – in possession of an ancient, rusty .38 special with an electrical tape cylinder and a broken hammer is nevertheless ready to pistol whip his way to family fame; he too, at 13 years of age hasn't seen a single white person on foot since he went to the state fair to watch that horse poop.

Every crew has to have a leader, and this crew has SamJai, who's convinced that the answer is to go bank a Jew. To get his plan of action okayed by the neighborhood patriarch is as simple as buying a miniature of Smirnoff and handing it to the wheel chair-bound man who is the brain trust of Lower Park Heights. Who better to advise the crew as to their raid up into Jew Town than Broke-Ass Rasheed?

The Sorrow of Broke-Ass Rasheed

Anno Domini 2023, Christmas Eve, Monday, December 25, 4:30 p.m., Park Heights and Belvedere, West Baltimore, Maryland

Since Nine and the SSH [Send Your Ass to Sinai Hospital] crew got done in by the Somali Famili over in Liberty Heights doing that bad deal, the Park Heights Crew had come on up, now dominating the corner:

At age 14, Snickarius Webb had a badass golden hoody trimmed in black and two razors stole from his skank-ass sisters. He didn't want to have nothing to do with no chump-ass drug dealing. Snickarius wanted reparations, plain and simple, recovered from any who had benefited from his sorry plight—which meant the whole world, so far as he saw it.

Jamalabad Johnson had his grandmamma's rusty-ass .38 snub-nose she stole from a cop she used to date way back in the ancient-ass day. He had no bullets for it and it would not fire no way, but it would be good for a pistol-whipping and what's a pistol-whipping without a pistol and what is more of a pistol than a revolver? He was in love with the idea of the revolver as the cowboy gun of the Old West, when black gunfighters ruled the white ranges and crackers hid in the mountains and fought Indians rather than fight the black gunfighters that won the West—and somehow had it all taken from them by whoever shut them back up in these crowded-ass places. At 13, Jamalabad looked up to his half-brother Snickarius in all things, and Snickarius said that Samjai was okay, so Jamalabad went along.

Samjai was so light-skinned he was damned near white, so made up for this color deficiency with a stronger sense of racial identification. If it had not been for the fact that all—whites and blacks included—agreed that black blood was so much stronger than white, that there was no such thing as a mixed-race person and that one drop of black made you all black, then Samjai might have been a conflicted person. But there was not a doubt among the hate-filled human family that black blood pumped more meaningfully through the bodily veins than cracker juice. He hated everything white, was beginning to identify as a Muslim based on his made-up name alone, and found it especially hurtful to both his Black and Muslim sides that the white race even had their own secret society, Jews, who lived just two miles or so out the way and needed to pay—for what remained unclear. But the fact that the people who ran the whole world from secret rooms lived two miles from where he suffered all the poverties of soul and body—in a world of their diabolical design—was too painfully ironic for him to process in any nonradical way.

The snow pattered wetly.

The splatting of distant tires sprayed sidewalks and curbs with slush.

The squeaking slap of their sneakered feet played tentatively on the snow-melting asphalt of the street.

Before the Liquor Mart sat Broke-Ass Rasheed, his Black Panther beret still in place, but his Nation of Islam vowl to abstain from drinking the Whiteman's devil juice a tarnished memory, as he mourned the death of Nine and his crew at the hands of the Somali Famili, drinking a forty, tears streaking his wizened cheeks, snot streaking his grizzled beard. The three militant youth sought guidance to lend purpose to their impulse to strike out at the society that had stricken them numb in the cradle of neglect which had been their fatherless lives. In the tattered, besmirched and sorrowful figure of Broke-Ass Rasheed they saw a touchstone, some pool of memory that might glorify their unknown fathers and set their sons on the road to conquest—the path of positive redemption, placing them on the sacred verge of "stepping the fuck up," the dream of feral youth the world over among the like ruins of all dying civilizations.

He looked up, seeing them standing there in the slushy gutter, like three would-be wise men before a mechanical manger occupied by an agent of despair and nodded his ascent to their silent entreaty. As a city bus narrowly missed running them over in that drear hour before dusk, they stepped up onto the sidewalk and gathered into a three-point crescent around him to hear the first words of wisdom ever directed toward them by a man, "You dumbass hoppers need to mind the power of a bus to run your asses over. If you shoppin' a lawsuit for yo mamma, you want to be hit by a two-door sedan, or better yet be on a bus that get hit. No never mind, this is your corner now, so it stands-to-reason you occupy this shit righteously instead of trifling in the gutter."

The Seven Shades of Rasheed

Snickarius, Jamalabad and Samjai gathered around the elder statesmen of Lower Park Heights, which, if you is a nigga, be a slight on your kind, as Upper Park Heights is down the way *below* and Lower Park Heights is up on that high hill. This was just another reminder of the rampant injustice implicit in the Black American experience.

Broke-Ass Rasheed was ancient, damned near sixty, some said, half gray of beard—almost like that Santa Claus faggot, who did all the Christmas work for white people—part white of hair, with one messed-up leg left to him strapped straight out in a steel-pole boot and the other messed-up leg gone—took by white doctors, which were well-known to practice on black folks so that they could be better at fixing up white people. He had big hands, puffy, blackened lips and sleepy-lidded eyes of the big brown kind. He dressed in a black beret jangling with trinkets, a black leather jacket, a lopsided pair of jean pants and a single black leather boot. Over his leg and up around his rounded belly lay a gray blanket, draped like a shroud of mourning. Broke-Ass Rasheed was usually down in the dumps. But today, even as he cried and drank he seemed up in spirit.

Samjai was new to the crew, wearing a 'Che Forever' shirt, the light-skinned slave rebel depicted wearing a beret—like Broke-Ass Rasheed's, minus the jangles—on the designer shirt. Getting a good look at the 'Liquor Mart Wiseman' for the first time, Samjai pointed to the man's hat and said, "Righteously militant, my brutha!"

Rasheed nodded and bumped fists with all three, Samjai last, who could not contain himself and embarrassed Snickarius and made Jamalabad roll his eyes as he ran off at the mouth, "Rasheed is a bad-ass name, also. But how'd you get stuck with Broke-Ass? Snickarius says it's 'cause you broke all the time and Jamalabad claims it 'cause your ass is actually broke from taking lead in it—like they shot your ass right here and there you sit!

Rasheed rolled his eyes, looked to the two experienced crew members and said, "I suppose it's about time ya'll young-ass niggas knew da trute. I need me a little drink though. So, if you be kind enough to get me a miniature of Smirnoff, Broke-Ass Rasheed will bring home the trute."

Taking a dollar bill out from under his blanket, he held it out to Samjai, who ran into the Liquor Mart, bought the mini, and brought it right back out to the handicapped old butha, who unscrewed the tiny top, sucked the thing dry and then tossed the plastic bottle in the gutter, declaring, "This ole soldia on the verge of a righteous deed. So if you young-ass niggas wants ta know how he got to the pinnacle of grace, gatha 'round and take in the Song of Broke-Ass Rasheed."

A <u>White</u> <u>Christmas</u>

Under the stuttering yellow light and the darkening sky, the three gathered like ghosts about a dying man in the driving snow, thirsty to feast upon his human essence as the light of life yet flickered.

"First, there were Cute-Ass Rasheed, Mamma's first hope, the apple of her EBT pie, the baby that brought home the bacon. Yeah, you know what I'm talkin' 'bout, damned-near-white as you is, Samjai. Sheeee, as light as you is Mamma was displayin' yo ass like White Daddy's own pearl necklace."

Snickarius and Jamalabad snickered and hooted at the singling out of the new cut of the crew.

"But then, as happens, when Baby's Daddy don't come 'round fo no second date, Mamma lays up with anotha nigga—en nine month's afta' that shiftless muthafucka's shoes hit the sidewalk, pop, here come Little Sista and don't you know, Cute-Ass Rasheed done got demoted to Bitch-Ass Rasheed—you know how it is Snick, yo ramen noodle money goin' to braids fo yo little sista.

"As happens, when a giant bitch mamma call her son a Bitch-Ass right out da cradle, he needs ta prove hisself—so he did, and became Whooped-Ass Rasheed—piled on by bigga kids, beat by the nigga that fuckin' his mamma and so on—you know it, Jamalabad, I saw yo sista's daddy trowin' you out da window twice now."

"Ya'll young-asses know it's true!"

To this the boys shuffled, nodded and hung their heads, feeling the plight of their elder as a child, each in his own way, according to his particular curse.

"Then, after some years of takin' whoopin, afta whoopin, Whooped-Ass Rasheed finds hisself halfway trough a can a spinach—which was all the shit his mamma let him eat—but don't you know, that shit brought on the hulk in his frame. As he squatted on the side of the tub, feasting on them cold, soggy leaves with the plastic fork, while Mamma en her man, en Little Sista all eatin' scrimps en cake on the couch, watching Wrestlmania—the hulk come on him.

Within two days Whooped-Ass Rasheed's little hands was growed out ta chump-hammas like y'all scrawny-ass niggas see right here!"

To this Broke-Ass Rasheed theatrically flexed his giant man-hands and the boys cheered and swayed to the story, making punching motions as they grinned sinisterly.

"Thus came Bad-Ass Rasheed outa da High Hood to tread the sissy-braided faggots of the worl under his heavy, Niked-up heels. He bust a nigga's nose here, knock out a white boy's teeth there, crack the rib of some limp-dicked teacher up in school—beatdown two muthafuckin' skank-ass bitches who tought dey was men in Upper Saint Clair. Bad-Ass Rasheed choked out Snitchy the Shoe-Shine man right on his box-stool at the Lexington Market—a nigga ta be reckoned with, don't you know!—and took that shoeshine spot fo his own self."

The boys were howling in exultation and dancing around, boxing the punk shadows that crept on by before the passing headlights.

Then the big hand of the man called a halt and he intoned sorrowfully, "But to every bad-ass comes his day a downfall. Don't you know it, but Bad-Ass Rasheed run into a heavy-handed negro named Poet— seven foot tall in his sneakers, head like a bowling ball, not a sneak punch you could name but he don't trow it! Though, as the worl turn, the conqueror of Bad-Ass did not strangle him on his box-stool throne, but set him on his knee—so to speak—and talked of things sublime, that the name Rasheed was a holy seed, that he was destined to serve the Holy Nation of Islam, under the Honorable Reverend Louis Farrakhan, in the ultimate struggle against the White Devil, and a lesson learned from some cracker fiddler player, that the Devil is best done in by trick, not by the brick. Thus marked the rise of Slick-Ass Rasheed, whose story is the key to understanding the plight of Broke-Ass Rasheed."

The now animate old man, fresh snot running over his brush-like mustache, tears dried white like chalk-patterned lightning strikes on his cheeks, brought out another dollar from under the blanket, then added another two it and called, "A mini of One-Fifty-One, my Oreo friend, if you please."

As Samjai took the bills he noticed that Snickarius was peeping under the blanket, as if trying to discern the amount of money therein.

The old man in the power chair called after him, "Slick-Ass Rasheed is the precursor of Broke-Ass Rasheed, the current and Sixth Shade of that martyr name—and you two snoopin' niggas here don't want to find out the Seventh Shade of Rasheed—mark dese Broke-Ass words…"

Samjai was ecstatic, that he had stumbled upon such a man, such a storyteller, a man that surely could connect him with his Muslim roots and might very well know what was up with the Jews, like where their mind-control machines were kept and if they really became doctors so that they could snip off pieces of baby junk and insert tracking devices.

All that Glitters is Bold

The Quest of Slick-Ass Rasheed

It was damned near dark in front of the Liquor Mart.

The dope-slinging hour was nigh but no fiends skulked 'round about waiting for their high.

The corner's crew was no more. All that stood in the dying day's sour light were three skinny-ass hoppers standing about the broken man in the chair as he sucked down a mini of Barcardi 151. They recoiled a bit as he missed the last sip, and licked out for the mind-numbing drop, instead, lapping up ancient snot.

They then came back to their story-eared senses and gathered 'round, only to see a five dollar bill emerge in the big, meaty hand, the deep voice turned to gravel, "That shit were good, but went down a bit thick at the end. Get me anotha en a Steel Reserve—bottle for chuggin' no can. Keep da dolla change..."

Samjai was on it, becoming fast friends with the Asian man behind the glass-encased counter.

Back out on the sidewalk, pocketing his well-earned dollar, Samjai held out the mini, which was dumped into the large bottle and then downed as one foul unit, noxious, white suds washing over the deep, leather-brown face—still failing to dislodge all of the heavy paste of snot from the scrub-pad mustache, glistening in the gray-streaked steel wool of the beard, seeming to wash away years of pain from the grizzled old countenance.

Then, like some mutherfucker from heaven shone the Light of the Lost African Ages on the brown face, a truck headlight momentarily blazed it with glory while making one of those turns that usually caused other drivers among the adults to cuss and beep—to which the bottle was flung to destruction on the curb, a mighty belch sounding before the Liquor Mart, Samjai barely avoiding a gelatinous drop of something with a bob of his big head.

Snickarius and Jamalabad were obviously impressed by this feat of drinking and nodded, as if they had come to the right place and all ears perked up as their storyteller drawled, "Y'all young-ass hoppers don't wanna to sling no dope like a straight-up, low-down nigga or carry no punk, Whiteman-bought sign—so you wants a life a high adventure!"

The boys were engaged again, pumping their fists in the air, grinning in expectation of Christmas deeds to be told of old.

"Then gatha 'round en hea' The Quest of Slick-Ass Rasheed en his fateful—dumb-as-dog-shit-no doubt—homeboy, Otis Poppleton, hardheadedest nigga in da hood..."

A gurgling echoed in the meaty throat, then an inward reaching cough of disgusting proportions, caused the listeners to back up just a little, as Broke-Ass Rasheed flung a lunger at a passing car, a feat of spitsmanship that legend would one day have it scored a direct hit on the windshield.

The story teller then returned sternly to his edifying subject.

"...Two far-farin' bruthas who took da Numba Five from Mondawmin all da way out ta Cedonia—in da white-ass Eastside—in the endless quest to recover reparations for fou-hundred years a woe, on the snowy night of December-Claus, nineteen-ninety-five. All dat glittered was bold dey been told..."

White Avenue and Marluth, December Sometin', 1995, Dark as all hell after Otis lost his watch...

Having laid out the field of heroic reparations operations, Broke-Ass Rasheed was overcome with a spasm, and lurched, swinging his chair toward the gutter.

"Taking a break fo da surprise chapter."

"What?" opined Jamalabad

"A course dere a surprise chapta' so no white man can steal dat shit en copyright it, Fool. I'll have a readymade eggnog ta settle dis belly. Here a twenty, keep da change, but bring me da big bottle!"

Snickarius snagged the bill and was in the Liquor Mart in a flash.

Samjai stood wondering how one told a story with a surprise chapter when it was his own story.

This joint to be continued [after Broke-Ass Rasheed is done throwing up in the gutter] in Otis Poppleton's Big Idea...

Otis Poppleton's Big Idea

[Surprise Chapter]

As in the days of King Arter and the Knights of the Black Table, you got Marvin your wizard and hardheaded thugs like Sir Jamalot, with Slick-Ass Rasheed basically your wizard in this case and Otis Poppleton the knight who forgot his Superman cape— S and all, left that shit in the closet.

A sign of things to come dawned on Slick-Ass Rasheed when the Number-Five—which they riding up into Cedonia—pass Frankford on Sinclair and Big Ben Witten had his Neked People sign out—meaning there'd be hos dancin' in his bar and Otis was all ready to misdirect the expedition for buy-one-get-one-free

Colt Forty-Five draft. But the Slick-Ass brains of the operation kept them to they gold, and before you know it they slinkin' up White Avenue lookin' for white people houses with no cars, because—and hear me now—if a white people house don't have a car in front, them folks is out and you can take they shit. This one particular house have promise—no car—so we creep around back and Slick-Ass see a free-standin' garage which was probably for all they fancy junk, but might have a car in it—but no!

There he is—Otis that is, 'cause Slick-Ass wouldn't do such a fool thing—down in the back stairwell, peering into a lit-up club basement at some fine-ass, buck-naked white woman laid out face down on a pool table, polishing the eight-ball in her little hands as if to see her reflection, like she waitin' on a brutha ta fall out of the sky.

Slick-ass, puts hands ta Otis' shoulders and says, "No, ma butha," and Otis is like, "Good, goog-a-moog—you see that. She been waitin' fo black Santa Claus too long."

"No, Otis, something ain't quite right."

"Shieed, nigga, you gay?"

"Be quiet!" hissed Slick-Ass.

"Shid, nigga, you hea' dat music roarin'? She can't hea' shit."

And before Slick-Ass could hold that heavy-boned brutha back, "crash," Otis kick in the door and Slick-Ass right behind him with hands on shoulders ready to prevent a rape charge coming up out of this and the woman don't even scream, but roll over and smile at them while the music cuts out and a loud click of a shotgun being pumped had them looking to their right, where one giant, hairy white man and one narrow, evil white devil be grinning like the cats that caught the mouse.

Actually, once the white woman rolled over she didn't look all that good. But that was the least of their worries. The narrow, bald, mean, white devil was fingering a Rambo knife and rolling his eyes while the giant dude was looking at Slick-Ass and Otis down the barrel of the biggest shotgun eva made!

Slick-Ass thought they was dead, then the big man smiled and said, "Hey Snit, are you thinking what I'm thinking?"

Then the little devil comes with, "Can't wait, Ronbone."

Then the woman raised an objectifying tone, "Oh no, Ron, you know I don't ride that dirt road."

The big hairy man laughed and leveled Otis with a butt-stroke of the shotgun and stepped on Slick-Ass so he bent like a blade of grass and laughed, "Not you, Kath—finish cuttin' the coke, will ya."

With that Slick-Ass was yanked to his feet and tied with cord and duct tape by the evil Snit cracker while the woman arranged lines of coke on her belly, which the giant man snorted, all greedy like. Before Slick-Ass knew it he was sitting on the couch next to the giant Ronbone cracker, whose feet—as big as bread boxes—was pinning Otis to the floor while he drank beer with his left hand and hugged Slick-Ass with his other giant arm and they watched the cracker named Snit snorting coke off of this lady's behind.

Otis done woked up about the time that Snit was finished snorting the powder out of the creases of that pasty white ass. Otis was dumber than usual after he woke. To begin with, Otis was not the sharpest knife in the drawer. But after Ronbone went upside his head with that gun butt, he wasn't even the sharpest spoon.

Then it comes, the death march of racism, those evil, white, muvafuckin' racists havin' baited the heroes of the quest with that false white pussy and takin' them to they doom. Up the stairs, hands tied and mouths taped, Otis and Slick-Ass went, the devil Snit prancing and cackling in front and the ugly white giant creaking the step boards behind. Then, as they was in the kitchen, the woman yelled from downstairs, "Hey, Hon, could you take out the crescent rolls. Mom and Dad are coming over and I need to get cleaned up."

The giant rumbled, "Sure, Kath," and did as she said, even handing a crescent roll to his friend, who gobbled it like a fiend. Stuffing they greedy, pale faces, they was then ushering Slick-Ass Rasheed and his booty-smitten sidekick:

Out into the cold, cruel night

At the mercy of all the evil that is white,

Toward an unmarked van of white,

To take those unlucky bruthas into the mad night.

Now don't count Slick-Ass Rasheed and Otis Poppleton out yet, 'cause they got one more chance fo redemption in What's in the Bag, the next-to-last verse in The Song of Broke-Ass Rasheed, the last being as yet unsung, making What's in the Bag the conclusion of the story of how a man comes to carry such a tragical name...

Overture: What's in the Bag?

Warm out-da-boddle eggnog chugged, flowing yellow ova da wooly bristle of beard and mustache as the boys looked on like devils at a penitent funeral.

"Ahh yeah. Where was I?"

"Bout ta buy a cartoon a smokes, yo," opined Snickarious Webb, pocketing three dollars and some change from the twenty he used to buy the drink for the elder storyteller in the sit-rolling chair."

Samjai corrected his set leader, "What's in The Bag—affer the two evil crackas grab Otis en Slick-Ass!"

Jamalabad nodded, seconding that motion and took an elbow in the ribs from Snickarious, as Broke-Ass Rasheed recovered his bardic composure with a towering belch that sprayed the boys in yellow droplets and forged on into the storied past under the yellowed light of the whining Liquor Mart sign, the pain of years gone by painted in mad dashes of brightness across his leathered and nog-besmirched face by the passing headlights.

"So Otis 'Gonna-ged-me-some-white-boody' Poppleton sat in sorry dismay, hands taped behind, next to Slick-Ass 'We-fuckeded-now' Rasheed, who, likewise taped hands behind, sat next to his dumb-as-dog-shit partner on the very same cracker toolbox dat dem babblin' niggas a ole must a used to build God's misunderstood Tower a Baffled Bitches."

Wincing at that bit of religious retrogression, the boys jolted back a step as Broke-Ass finished the unsavory baby milk drink for old drunks, belched thunderously and forged on with wide, clear eyes, like some TV nigga who finally see the monster in the movie that about to kill him...

"Den let the sorry-ass story be told!"

Continued in Epiphany: What's in the Bag, soon as Broke-Ass Rasheed geds his drink on...

Epiphany: What's in the Bag?

The crazy-eyed, crazy cracker named Snit squatted behind the ensnared heroes, an arm over each shoulder, grinning from ear-to-ear, his face like to split, as he looked from one to the other and the van rolled on into the snowy night. Through the woods, over the hills and into the nary-real night they rolled, bobbing and bouncing uncomfortable-like on that tool box, the grinning head of the White Devil bobbing between them, and the broad, hairy back of that afro-headed sasquatch mutherfucker drove like the greatest devil of them all was on their tail. While this monstrosity did drive, he with his evil minion, did contrive:

"Hey, Snit," it rumbled, hands hairy-white on the wheel, "ready for a riddle?"

"Sure, Ronbone!"

"Okay, Snit, how do you keep a nigger from drowning?"

"That's easy, Ronbone. You bone him and gut him and fit him with a compressed air bladder for flotation—best wetsuit a scuba queer ever dove for pearls with."

"Wrong," roared Ronbone. "One more chance or I make you practice on your new friends and we won't get to play What's in the Bag with Douchebag Diesel.

As Ronbone split a pair of headlights with his own and drove some poor motorist off the road into the woods, Snit worked his leathery white jaw in the lurid glow of the dashboard lights, and unable to reach his own head, scratched Otis' head in consternation, seeming to wrack his pea brain for the answer. "Come on, 'Bone, I was jus' gettin' used ta ownin' me a boy!"

Ronbone rumbled beastlike, "You dumb fucking hillbilly, you get one more chance to answer correct or we carve up your nigger."

"Well, which one is mine, I'd like to know," simpered Snit, like a baby living under threat of taken candy.

Ronbone laughed like the Archfiend his own self, sped up, veered slightly to the side to destroy a mailbox made like a gingerbread house with the right fender and then declared, "The dumb nigger is yours, Snit. Just like whores, you get the dumb bitch and I get the one who figures out she's not making it home before its obvious!"

Otis began to throw up and the Snit devil grabbed him, slid open the side door and held his big head out in the rushing snow-flecked air of the night as Otis hurled.

Ronbone then looked in the rearview mirror at Slick-Ass and said, "We're just having fun, Bro. We'll have you home in your ghetto shack in just over an hour."

As Broke-Ass contemplated the fact that this Ronbone devil was smarter then him and knew he was going to look into that rearview mirror when he did, the joking started a fresh, "So, Snit, one last time or I make you throw your boy from the van so I can paint the mud flaps red."

"Ready, Ronbone!" snapped the frightening Snit.

Ronbone then looked into the mirror as he destroyed another mailbox—this one with a Santa Clause on it—and said, "How do you keep a nigger from drowning?"

"Shit, 'Bone, that's easy, you take your foot off the back of his head!"

"Give that man a drink," said the giant, as he handed back a bottle of Jack Daniels and the sour smell made Ortis sob and the giant laughed as the Snit man danced in a squat and guzzled, flashing wicked eyes first to one then to the other as the van took a hard right turn up a hill so big it seemed a mountain, the Whiteman's Wicked Mountain, from where He rules the cruel world and those sorry folks caught up in it's cold embrace, foremost among them our devil-taken race.

Up and up the monster-driven van crawled, white in the night, taking Slick-Ass Rasheed—who were not feeling too slick just then—and that booty-smitten fool, Otis 'Dumbass' Poppleton to a ron-dee-view with their own messed-up plight.

Then, soon as the snow-blowing White Devil took a breath, our zero and our hero found themselves parked at a crossroad.

To the back was the way they came, up the windy road.

To the right was a dirt road to a farm, where Slick-Ass imagined they would be buried.

To the left was a gravel road into a woods, where Otis imagined they'd be lynched.

Straight ahead was a new road, winding up and up to a big house on the top where the road ended. On either side of the road was another big house, making three big houses in all, the two to each side all decorated with Christmas lights, the one on the hilltop dark and foreboding.

Ronbone turned off the van and turned—a great, hulking shadow in the wintery night—and produced a bag. To which Snit, smacking his lips from a drink, said, "What's in the bag?"

Ronbone then opened the little bag and pulled some things that were bent up out of the bag and placed one on Otis' head and another on Slick-Ass, as if he were an albino King Kong dressing up bitches at the beauty supply super-store. They looked at each other in amazement and saw that they were dressed in elf ears.

As if in answer to their unspoken question of mind, Ronbone said, "They're green. Sorry. Didn't know we'd have nigger elves."

Snit was jumping up and down in a squat with his hand on Otis' shoulder and his bottle of Jack spilling on Slick-Ass, which brought a scolding from Ronbone, "Watch the whiskey, Snit."

Snit calmed down, snorting in a snickering way, his sour breath on their back as Ronbone spoke. "Gentlemen, we have three houses here, all customers of mine. There is Rebar Grantland, a mercenary and big game hunter who is heavy into pain meds ever since he fell out of a chopper shooting a cape buffalo. He's a good dude, good customer. If you manage to stumble into his place—have fun with that. We don't recommend it. If you get into his place he'll consider it a favor from us, save him the trouble of buying a nigger tag from the fish and game commission. In that case, you and us are square."

Otis' eyes got gigantic and he shook his head, as if trying to clear it.

The giant continued in a hushed tone, "Then there is Doctor Wallenstein, who fucked up Kathy's boob job. He's a faggot. Don't hurt him, just clean out his safe and we'll split it with you—bang his wife if you want. The damned Jew married one of you, if you can believe that shit. If it comes to him calling the cops, just tell him you know he has two keys of coke in his attic."

"And there is Mary and Steve 'Douchebag' Diesel. Mary buys from us, pays with blow jobs. Her husband is a little sissy, stays in the basement all night playing videogames. Snit and I make deliveries while the idiot is screaming at the TV in the basement. Douchebag is loaded. If you could scare Mary into opening his safe, we'll split the cash with you. You can't hurt her—we like her. If you have sex with her— the deal's off and in the river you go.

"So, if you two homeboys succeed in getting whacked by Rebar, robbing Wallenstein—optionally banging his old lady—or ripping off Steve, without touching Mary, then we're hunky-dory, we split the money with you—unless you're mounted over Rebar's fireplace—drive you back to your roach motel and forgive you for breaking my basement door. The way I see it you have a two-out-of-three chance of walking away from your night of misadventure the richer for your trouble."

Otis and Slick-Ass frantically nodded, "Yes" and they soon found themselves being un-taped and pushed up the darkened country road toward the three houses, a low snicker of devilish tone cackling behind them as they lurched uneasily into the night and up the hill, stiff-legged and elf-eared, on mutherfucking Christmas Night.

Exodus: What's in the Bag?

The Song of Broke-Ass Rasheed #4.8

And so they stood under the dandruff sky, in the fading glow of the van lights as it backed up, our slick-ass hero, Rasheed and our dumbass zero, Otis. The lights and noises of the van soon faded into the distance as they contemplated the situation.

The big, brooding house on the hilltop was definitely where the hunter lived—no, sir, not even Otis were that dumb.

A White Christmas

The house to the left had a Beamer and a Cadillac parked in the driveway—definitely where the rich man lived.

The house to the right, where the coke ho lived, had a Buick and a Nissan out front.

The choice was clear, take the house on the left by going up the back deck and breaking in, quiet-like.

Signaling to each other with their fingers and pointing to shit in the snow-speckled dark made them feel like commandos in some movie, and before they knew it they were standing on the back deck looking into a bedroom with a giant curtained bed and all kinds of girly things decorating the dresser. Otis' eyes got big as he saw all of the jewelry laid out on the long dresser with the big mirror and the strange little chair in front of it that was pulled out like somebody had just been sitting there.

Otis' eyes got big over the jewels, rings, bracelets, necklaces and hooped earrings as big as a pie plate!

Slick-Ass was somewhat worried over the chair seeming to have recently held an occupant and began making the commando sign for not going the fuck in just yet. But when he turned to look at Otis that dumbass was already heading through the decorative glass door, which had not even been locked. As Otis walked wide-eyed toward the jewels Slick-Ass Rasheed was behind him whispering, "Sometin ain' right, Yo!"

Otis turned and shushed him with a scowl and then Slick-Ass Rasheed, looking over Otis' shoulder at the movement his keen-ass eyes caught, saw, to his astonishment, the tallest, biggest, well-built sister a brutha could even imagine. I mean this bitch was NBA-big, was bald, out a her wig, which was on a robot head on the long dresser, wearing a fine purple dress and high heels, and throwing a karate kick right into Otis' belly—and the brutha went down!

Slick-Ass Rasheed then found himself standing over his fallen partner, who was curled up in agony, as this towering, monster bitch pointed one long-ass finger in his face, a finger tipped with a two inch sharp fingernail, one big man hand on her giant hip and her big watermelon head bobbling as she hissed, "Little nigga, if I weren't headed out to get me some strange dick I'd be kickin' holes in that soft head a yours! What da fuck you think you doin' up in here in my fuckin' crib? You one a dem jealous niggas? A sister land her a pencil-dicked midget Jew and make good en some hood nigga got a pop his nappy head up outa da sewer en try ta tarnish dat shit—hugh, huh? You listenin' to me, boy? Is you a hood nigga come to skulk on Aretha just 'cause she scored a white man?"

Slick-Ass Rasheed stood up on his tippy-toes and gave his slickest smile ever and said, "I told him not to, Miss. I was trying to stop his ass. Really, we was supposed to take a message to a white bitch named Marry—we just got the wrong house—we good dudes, really we are."

Her big eyes, one pretty and brown and the other scary and green, seemed to bore through his eyes and into his brain as she wagged that finger—and let me tell you little niggas, that finger could a scooped out an eye ball—in the face of Rasheed and then seemed to remember something, straightened up, noticed her bra was in disarray, tucked one giant titty back in its sling, crossed her arms, curled her lip and said, "Get da fuck out, negro and take this fat muvafucka with you—go on, before I change my mind and fuck up this new dress. Roughest part about bein' with a rich white man—a bitch always gotta look her best, en dese kina clothes ain't no good fo whoopin ass—shit, a bitch go upside a nigga's head and flop, there goes a titty. A bitch put some back-talkin' bitch at the CVS in a headlock, en pop, there go a seam that can't be mended with no normal thread—now ged da fuck out 'fo I tax yo chump ass!"

At that particular point in time Slick-Ass Rasheed temporarily became Strong-Ass Rasheed and dragged ole Otis out a harm's wicked way, out the door, down the stairs and into the darkened yard.

They were soon hobbling away from the house across the street to the supposed white lady house,

Otis getting his breath back and moaning, "Whad da fuck, yo? Dat was the biggest bitch dis nigga eva seen!"

Slick-Ass corrected that shit, "Shieed, Ma Nigga that was Dennis Rodman in drag!"

Now, on the side of the supposed white lady house, Otis crinkled up his face and whispered real loud, "Slick-Ass, I gots ta shit."

"What, is you stupid?"

"Slick-Ass, she done kicked da shit out a me—it's about ta blow—I gots ta go."

"Okay, it's natural—just somewhat inconvenient. Use these here bushes en I'll keep guard by the corner of the house—make sure that evil bitch is really goin' out."

"Ma Main Man," declared Otis, "I'll be right as rain in no time."

A <u>White</u> <u>Christmas</u>

As Otis squeezed between the side-of-the-house-fancy-bushes, Slick-Ass spied on that monster bitch's house and sure enough, there she go, marching out to the Cadillac, flopping down in that thing and speeding off to whatever kind a man could handle all of that. Then, as the sound of her car eased away, he heard Otis whisper, "Yo, Slick-Ass, I needs some help."

Slick-Ass hissed back, "Are you kiddin' me nigga?"

"Brutha," said Otis, "Dat big ole bitch stepped on my hand en its brokeded!"

Slick-Ass then did the unthinkable, unbuckled a nigga's belt en pulled down his pants, before returning to his lookout post, Otis grunting and whatnot in the background. Then, after the man had his moment, Otis called fo help getting his pants back up amid such an undesirable stench as a man never want to be called upon to deal with again.

"Oh, thank you, Ma Brutha," said Otis, and hero and zero skulked on to the back of the house, up onto the deck, past a bedroom window and to a sliding glass door that opened into a big living room—and lo and take hold, don't you know rich crackers in Richland don't even lock they back doors and in they went. As soon as they got in they heard the thunder of explosions and other movie sounds coming from the basement, all the way up through the main floor. So they knew that the big hairy man had been correct and that some crazy goof sat below in his basement playing video games while the wife remained neglected upstairs, down the narrow hall to the right.

Otis slinked behind, letting Slick-Ass take the risk, and so the hero did, walking flat into that bedroom, to find a fine, tall white lady in nice white-lady clothes, emptying a shopping bag on her bed. She looked at them, got a scared look on her face, and then exchanged it for a sly grin and asked, "Are you friends of Ronbone?"

"I thought so," she grinned, "What will it be?"

"Oh," says Slick-Ass Rasheed, "Mister Ronbone wanted us to pick up some money for him. He was pressed for time and was unable to enjoy your company."

A dark look shadowed her eyes, then she forced a smile and said, "The usual pickup?"

"Yes, ma'am," said Slick-Ass, too slick-like.

To this she snarled with a crazy look in her eyes, and dumped out the CVS bag, which had lubricant and a giant box of giant-sized condoms in it and spat, "So big Ron's busy with Kathy, huh, and sends the B-team. Is that it?"

She stormed out of the room.

Otis and Slick-Ass looked at each other nervously and Otis said, "She is a fine bitch—white beside. Maybe we get some pussy?"

"How stupid can one nigga be!" hissed Slick-Ass, "that dude will kill us, 'in the river' he said."

Otis just shrugged his shoulders, "You know how it is, Yo. It's my duty to service that booty. Besides, after that big bitch kicked my belly in I'd like some tender touchin.'"

The woman, Margaret, he thought her name was, came back into the room and handed Slick-Ass a bundle of 20-dollar bills as big as a brick, then ran her fingers around his neck and sat cross legged on the bed and looked up at both of them, saying in a husky voice, "Well, boys?" she said, licking her lips seductively and grinning sideways.

Slick-Ass said, "Thank you very much, miss." And out the door and down the hall he went, hoping not to run into a crazy videogame insane man, made his way out through the door, onto the deck and down the stairs. Noticing that Otis wasn't behind him he walked over into the grass enough that he could see up into the sliding glass door, deciding to give Otis a ten count before he went back in and got him.

Meanwhile, in the den of the evil crackers, dumbass Otis Poppleton was mesmerized by this fine white lady in brown hair, batting her eyes and handing the box of King Kong condoms to him. Otis didn't know quite how to let the lady down and stood confused as to what should be said. She took this for a cute moment and stood up, real close to him, beginning to take her skirt off, so it was now or never and Otis blurted, "Miss, I'll have to ask you for the regular kind 'cauz, you know, it ain't all dat."

"That's okay, Baby," she purred and gave him a big juicy kiss on his fat lips—and if you must know— Otis was one ugly dude. But that kiss was mighty heartfelt and had Otis under her spell as she stepped back, her long, thin, pale arms resting momentarily on his round brown shoulders and said, with a wink and a smile, "Really, it's okay Sugarbear—they aren't for you."

And, having said that weird shit she pulled up her skirt and Otis saw that she was really a dude! A dude that looked like he could do some damage at that!

So dumbass Otis, having failed to heed Slick-Ass Rasheed tore through the house, ran out the door and did not turn to go down the stairs, he was running so heavy and fast and plowed right through the deck railing and squashesd Slick-Ass Rasheed, breaking his fucking back and landing him in this metal chair—as Broke-Ass Rasheed.

The boys stood dumfounded, then Snickarius laughed harshly and Jamalabad took a step back. Only Samjai now seemed to be interested in the history of Broke-Ass Rasheed, "So what happened to Otis?"

Broke-Ass Rasheed was now drunk with despair, "Oh, his fat ass was fine since Rasheed broke his fall! He turned over a new leaf after that close call and is now the minister at Greater Peace Ministries Church over on Frederick Road."

Samjai touched the back of Broke-Ass Rasheed's hand, the leathery paw cracked with gray seams between the darkening brown in this cold night. "I'm sorry. How about if I just call you Rasheed?"

Broke-Ass Rasheed seemed a little choked up over that and nodded "yes" with his eyes. Then Snickarius had another question...

I'm Too Goddamn Old

The Song of Broke-Ass Rasheed #5, Conclusion

Samjai really felt for old Rasheed—the broken dude having had such a hard life. But Snickarius and Jamalabad just wanted to find out about the dice spot behind the liquor store, where legend had it Broke-Ass Rasheed used to spin dice better than anybody and knew the lucky spot on the curb. Rasheed kept begging off, saying, "Naw, naw, naw—it weren't all that. Besides, I'm too goddamn old to rumple-stumple this buggy back there over all that broken block."

The boys would not take no for an answer and helped Rasheed guide his power chair back behind the liquor store, clearing a path through the gap in the broken wall, onto an old parking pad—for like horses and wagons or some shit, it was so banged up and crumpling. Finally they came to the dice spot, a chalked-off slab of pavement in near pristine condition, up against the intact curb, against the completely crumbled sidewalk the liquor store man used to haul his trash. Thing was, that liquor store man respected the Park Heights Boyz to such an extent that he did not dare tread on the curb or the spot where dice were spun, and so this place of gambling was like a sacred precinct—actual concrete that wasn't crumbling apart.

"This sho is the spot. So what you young hoppers needs ta know?"

"We need ta know how much money you be given us so we don' whoop yo broke ass—ya ole fool nigga!" snarled Snickarius, as he pointed his broken gun at Rasheed's face, pointing the finger of his other hand at the blanket under which Rasheed kept his money. Not to be outdone, Jamalabad pulled out both of his straight razors and placed one up under the old man's eye.

Samjai was aghast and snatched up a brick, but no attention was paid to him. His friends had so little regard for him and his stature among them that they paid him no heed and had not even consulted with him about doing this rotten thing.

"No!' said Samjai.

Jamalabad simply gave him an evil stare.

Rasheed was not flustered, "You some real lowdown niggers ain't you?"

In answer Snickarius slammed the barrel of his little broke gun into the face of the broke man and Jamalabad pressed the razor so it made a trickle of blood on that big brown cheek, the light from the backdoor security camera glinting off of both blades, including the other, which was held at the ready to go for the throat.

"Give it!" snarled Snickarious, as blood trickled from the nose of Broke-Ass Rasheed.

Rasheed answered, clear-toned and even, "Here I thought you hoppers had a chance to become somethin'—even spared yer asses the story of the sixth shade, not wantin' to infect a young mind with the taint of mine."

Snickarius was snarling, "You pluckin' my las' nerve, niggar! Give it!"

With that command Jamalabad placed his second razor on the Rasheedian throat, the other still bleeding the cheek under the eye.

"Sho lille brutha. Jus' say da word," capitulated Rasheed.

"Whazyougot unda dere—unda dat blanket?"

A <u>White</u> <u>Christmas</u>

Rasheed grinned a triumphantly unbroken smile and sneered, "Say hello to my little friend!"

With that, a loud pop sounded and blood darted from under Jamalabad's chin, his one eye rolling out and hanging on a gooey red string as he tilted back and gurgled, falling and slicing his own face with the razors as his confused hands grabbed for his hanging eye.

Broke-Ass Rasheed had a dark light in his narrow eyes and Snickarius—not so bad sounding now—took a step back and stammered a word that never came out, but began with a "w," as Rashhed threw aside the blanket with his left hand, money flying everywhere and pointed a little gun at Snickarius and sneered, "You done summoned up Evil-Ass Rasheed en that muthafucka's a bad seed!"

"Pop" went the gun and a burst of blood blew out of Snickarius' ear and he fell straight back, eyes wide open, a red dot between them.

Rasheed and Samjai then met with their eyes over the body of Snickarius and the man spoke, nodding at the brick in Samjai's little hand, "I appreciate the thought. But you got better things to do with your fresh life than to get involved in this nastiness. Now I got bidness to up-end to, so if you could cast that blanket back ova my lap, I'd much appreciate that shit."

Without dropping his sacred brick—that somehow felt like his defining possession—Samjai placed the blanket back on the man's big lap and noticed an arsenal. Strapped to Rasheed's right leg, it's barrel taped to the inside of his iron-booted shoe, was a big-ass shotgun. On his lap was an Uzi and now also the little pistol as Rasheed helped Samjai cover up his hands, the left one peeking out to operate the control box for the chair. It occurred to Samjai then, that power chairs should be right-handed and Rasheed laughed a big toothy grin at the look on his face where his thoughts were so obviously etched, "That's right, son, Evil-Ass rides customized. Now get on out da way and home to your mamma, 'cuz Evil-Ass Rasheed got some bidness to un-tend."

Rasheed then cruised through the gap in the wall, leaving Samjai with his two dead friends and the boy just had to follow, brick in hand, after his very own man-defining hero."

"Wait, yo," he said as he caught up with Rasheed in front of the liquor stores as a big car full of Somalis with their triangular garlic-bulb heads rolled up almost to the curb and started piling out, drawing guns big and small.

Rasheed shoved Samjai to the ground and yelled, "Run!" as he opened up with the shotgun, with one hand while he lifted up the blanket-covered Uzi with the other. The flaming "blam" blasts of the shotgun that kept blamming and the machinegun sound of the Uzi and the pops of the Somali guns, the shattering of Somali car windows, the blasting of the liquor store windows and the terrible howling of Evil-Ass Rasheed, who only said one long-ass word for the whole gunfight, rose to a crescendo, the call of Rasheed somehow louder than the gunfire as he howled, "Muthafuckaaaaasssssssss…"

Within seconds it was over, four dead Somali dudes, one real dead car, one Somali man standing over the old man chair, and Rasheed, broken again, gurgling from a hole in his neck as he squeezed triggers that clicked empty, still attempting to curse up at his killer, who held a wicked-looking handgun before his forehead, smiling like he knew he was the bad guy and he got to win in the movie anyhow.

Samjai screamed, "No!" as he lunged forward and threw that brick overhead with both hands into the surprised mouth of the man turning to face him, a face you'd thought would make a cracking sound, as it was so bony-looking, but made a squishing sound instead. The man fell back like a falling trashcan in the winter wind, an empty look in his eyes, and when the back of his head cracked on the pavement like a watermelon dropped off the Fireworks Day table, the wicked looking gun clattered on the sidewalk as lifeless as its owner.

Samjai stepped to Rasheed's side and looked into his red, watery eyes, not wanting him to die. Rasheed took a finger that was not shot off and plugged the hole in his throat and rasped wetly, "See who da nigga is—I gots ta know fo I go."

Samjai scrambled, in a panic that he would not be able to honor his hero's last request and hauled out a wallet from the back jean pocket of the man with the squished face and the cracked head. He bounced right up as sirens sounded in the distance, opened up the wallet and bugged his eyes out at what he saw, but did his duty of holding the open wallet up before the dying eyes of his friend, who did not seem as surprised as one might expect that the Somali man was a Baltimore City Police Detective.

Rasheed looked at Samjai, smiled, which caused more blood to squirt from the throat hole, then managed to plug it with his thumb and rasped, "Ma hero, Cop-Jacker Jay—now get gone—" and the gurgling became something unpluggable by the big thumb of Rasheed and the converging police sirens sounded closer, inspiring freshly minted Cop-Jacker Jay to get good and gone...

Morning found him waking from among the steamy leaves of the old leaf heap behind Cylburn Conservatory for White Peoples' Pretty Flowers, the shimmering, orange dawn, assuring him that a future of infamous promise awaited his young-ass.

The End